MANSA MUSA

THE MOST FAMOUS AFRICAN TRAVELER TO MECCA

BARBARA KRASNER

New York

Published in 2017 by The Rosen Publishing Group, Inc.
29 East 21st Street, New York, NY 10010

First Edition

Library of Congress Cataloging-in-Publication Data

Names: Krasner, Barbara, author.
Title: Mansa Musa : the most famous African traveler to Mecca /
Barbara Krasner.
Description: New York : Rosen Publishing, [2017] | Series: The Silk
Road's greatest travelers | Includes bibliographical references and
index.
Identifiers: LCCN 2015047935 | ISBN 9781508171515 (library bound)
Subjects: LCSH: Musa, Sultan of Mali, active 1324—Juvenile literature.
| Muslim pilgrims and pilgrimages—Africa—Juvenile literature. | Mali
(Empire)—Kings and rulers—Biography—Juvenile literature.
Classification: LCC DT532.2.M87 K73 2015 | DDC
966.2/017092—dc23
LC record available at http://lccn.loc.gov/2015047935

Manufactured in China

CONTENTS

Since the time of the pharaohs, Africa has represented a land of riches that has attracted explorers, conquerors, and various other interlopers. Competition for this wealth—especially the thriving sub-Saharan gold trade that began in the fourth or fifth century—was often fierce. Between the ninth and sixteenth centuries, three kingdoms in the western Sudan, whose growth was nurtured in large part by the gold and salt trades, ultimately came to dominate these trades. In time, these kingdoms each evolved into a great empire. Thus arose the Ghana, Mali, and Songhay empires.

Ghana, the "kingdom of gold," most likely originated in the seventh century. By the ninth century, it had developed into an empire northwest of the present country of Ghana. It occupied the land now occupied by Senegal and southern Mauritania. The empire's wealth was based on gold and gold trade. When new goldfields emerged to the east, Ghana lost its trade. In the thirteenth century, Ghana also became the target of attacks from invaders. Mali had been a subservient kingdom, and its king served as a councilor to Ghana's king. When the kingdom of Ghana fell, Mali rose to power.

Mansa Musa established Islam as Mali's official religion. His beliefs led him to his famous trek across Africa to Mecca in 1324.

The empire of Mali probably originated in the tenth century and began to flourish around the thirteenth. In the course of its three hundred or so years of prominence, various individuals came to power. However, two of Mali's rulers, both black Muslims, are especially notable. In 1230 or so, Sundiata, an exiled Malinke prince, returned to his people at their request and achieved victory over the Sosso people, who had oppressed the people of Mali. He brought the various Malinke chiefdoms together under single rule. Eventually, Mali's size grew to nearly 500,000 square miles (1.3 million square kilometers).

Sundiata established the foundations of the Mali Empire, but it was a later successor who would cause the name Mali to reach far and wide. More than fifty years after Sundiata's reign, his brother's grandson succeeded him to the throne in 1312. Musa I, known as Mansa Musa (*Mansa* means "king of kings"), would be known as the richest and most noble king in all the land, richer than a billionaire in today's world.

While a Mali king long before him had con-verted to Islam, it was Mansa Musa who gave Mali an Islamic outlook and universal fame. When Mansa

Musa undertook his famed pilgrimage to Mecca in 1324, traversing parts of the routes that once made up the trading routes of the storied Silk Road, tales of his wealth reached several Arab travelers, who recorded what they heard.

Over the course of his journey, Mansa Musa visited new places and met new people. Although his enormous generosity and lavish spending devastated the economy of Cairo, Egypt, and forced him to borrow, he remained widely beloved. In Mali, he became a favorite of Muslim writers, who inscribed what they heard and recorded the oral traditions that were so important in Mali. They are largely responsible for what we know of him today.

On his return journey to Mali, Mansa Musa visited Timbuktu and Gao. After acquiring these cities for his empire, he developed them into bustling centers of trade and culture and brought Islamic architecture and learning to his broader empire.

Countries benefit from strong leadership such as Mansa Musa's. But weaker leaders ascended to the throne following his death, and the Mali Empire disintegrated into smaller chiefdoms—essentially becoming what it was two centuries before. Power then shifted to the empire of Songhay.

Still, Mansa Musa has endured as a pivotal figure for his role in transforming Mali's cultural and religious heritage. Moreover, he served as a cultural ambassador and international figure at a time when few journeyed outside the borders of their kingdoms. Throughout Mali today, the mosques he built with his architect, es-Saheli, remind us of Mansa Musa's vision and commitment to his people and his faith. Long after he was gone, his mark on Mali and the world remained.

CHAPTER ONE

THE SILK ROAD AND THE SPREAD OF ISLAM

• • • • • • • • • • • • •

The Silk Road was a system of commercial trade routes that linked peoples from China to the Mediterranean Sea. It crossed areas that lie in present-day China, Afghanistan, Turkey, Uzbekistan, and the Middle East, with some routes in India, Pakistan, and Mongolia. The Silk Road trade started more than a thousand years before Mansa Musa's time. The trade of silk and spices dominated the Silk Road, but many other goods were traded as well, and countless cultural exchanges facilitated the spread of ideas and technologies. Minerals such as gold and silver also were exchanged along the Silk Road. Both overland and sea routes made the trading possible.

The heyday of the Silk Road had largely passed by the time of Mansa Musa's rule in Mali in the

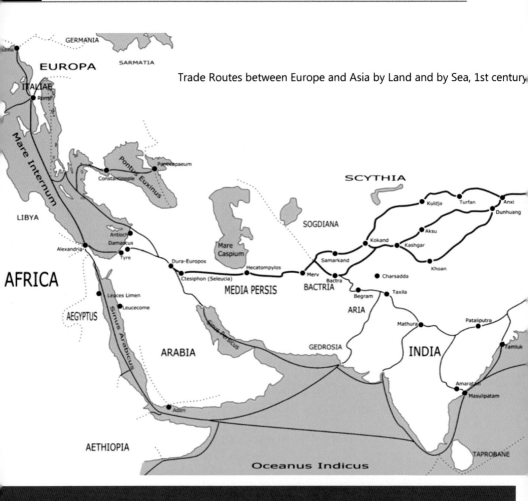

Trade Routes between Europe and Asia by Land and by Sea, 1st century

Trade routes, such as the Silk Road, helped to establish the path for the spread of Islam and the foundation of the gold trade.

fourteenth century. Still, the Silk Road had laid the path for cultural exchange, shared learning, and the expansion of the Islamic faith. It also laid the foundation for the development of the sub-Saharan gold trade.

THE SILK ROAD TURNS TO GOLD

Silk, of course, was the main product traded on the Silk Road. For centuries, the secrets of silk production did not spread beyond the boundaries of China, which meant China was the only source of the world's silk until around the sixth century CE. This made silk a valuable commodity in distant lands. China opened up trade routes to the West around the second century BCE, and after the first century BCE, the luxurious fabric was in high demand in the Roman Empire. In the West, silk was especially desired for use by royalty or the church. Even after Western lands acquired knowledge of silk production, however, trade of numerous other items continued to flourish along the Silk Road.

In addition to the trading of goods along the Silk Road, there was also the exchange of language, cultural practices and traditions, technologies, and scientific knowledge. Knowledge of paper making spread from China while travelers from India shared the decimal system. Arab contributions to medicine, philosophy, and algebra were also imparted over the Silk Road.

And then there was gold, exchanged in bars or bags of dust. Trade routes began to develop south to the Sudan to take advantage of rich gold sources. The gold brought settlement of commercial towns. The gold in these towns in turn attracted Muslim Sudanese traders.

The Silk Road reached its peak around the second century CE, but it continued to be a popular trade

Kirina was one of the major towns in Mali under Sundiata's rule. It was here where Sundiata defeated the Sossos. These structures in present-day Kirina store grain and keep it dry.

route through the Middle Ages. It suffered a period of decline, but the Mongols helped it rebound in the thirteenth and fourteenth centuries, until travel by sea became the preferred method.

THE RISE OF A NEW RELIGION

In the seventh century CE, a new religion called Islam gave Arab tribes a rallying cry, and they set out to conquer lands in order to spread their faith. Conquered lands included present-day Iraq, Iran, Syria, Palestine, Egypt, northern Africa, and Spain. Arab armies also invaded central Asia, western India, and even—although briefly—France. The Persian Empire vanished and the Byzantine Empire lost much of its power. The new rulers established a caliphate, or Islamic empire. The empire was anything but stable, and it eventually broke apart into smaller ruling geographic areas. No longer under the control of a single ruler, Islamic religion and culture were now able to reach remote areas. Along with the spread of Islam came trading routes and networks, penetrating present-day Eurasia, northern Africa, the eastern African coast, and parts of western Africa. Art and learning prospered.

In the eleventh century, there were two kingdoms in the western African areas of the Sudan—the Do and Malel. These two kingdoms were two of the early chiefdoms that developed among the Malinke people, the people who would later comprise the kingdom of Mali. (The name "Mali" means "where the king lives." "Mande" is a variant form of Mali; both "Mandingo" and "Malinke" mean "the people of Mali.") At some point, a Malel king converted to Islam. Subsequently, Islam became an important element of trade.

Barmandana, the first Muslim king of Mali, was said to have been converted in 1050 by a Muslim trader living in his kingdom. Barmandana had been told that belief in Allah would end a severe drought. Islam continued to be practiced by Malinke rulers, but it would still be some time before Islam became widespread in the region.

Muslim traders traveled to areas ruled by Islamic leaders. They soon overtook much of the Silk Road. Mosques and tombs of Islamic saints peppered the routes. They became places for weary Muslim travelers to rest. Hostels were built to accommodate the travelers and their beasts of burden. Even in places where Islam was not the dominant religion, such as China and India, Islamic religious institutions welcomed the Muslim traders. Islamic architecture developed even in central Asian cities, including Bukhara and Samarkand (both in present-day Uzbekistan), making new landmarks along the Silk Road. The Persian language, with some Arabic, spread to the East and became an official Islamic tongue and the language of the Silk Road.

THE RISE OF THE EMPIRE OF MALI

The Empire of Mali grew from the state of Kangaba, which had become home to the Malinke people by 1000 CE. The Malinke people served as middlemen in the gold trade in Ghana. When that empire splintered, the Malinkes became oppressed by Sumanguru Kante, the chief of another Mande people called the Sossos.

Kangaba would become Mali—and an empire— around 1230, under Sundiata, also known as Mari Diata. Sundiata, of the Keita clan, was an exiled prince from a Malinke chiefdom on the Sankarani, a tributary of the Upper Niger River. His people called him back to remove them from the grasp of Sumanguru. Sundiata tried to unite the various Malinke chiefdoms. Oral tradition, which ran strong in the kingdoms, told of a large battle that followed, in which each side

KANGABA

Sundiata came from a line of rulers from the small Mandingo state of Kangaba, which was on the Upper Niger River. After the conversion to Islam, Kangaba expanded to the south and southeast. The expansion invited the wrath of the Sossos. Sundiata achieved victory over them in battle at Kirina. He named Kangaba as the meeting place between him and the Malinke chieftains. At the Mandeblo sacred shrine, they swore their loyalty to Sundiata. Instead of an alliance of independent chiefdoms, Mali became an empire ruled by the Keita clan, with chiefdoms that depended on each other.

Kangaba, along the Niger River, became a sacred center for the Keita dynasty. In the 1920s, when two archaeologists collected oral traditions, they learned that Kangaba continued to serve as a sacred center. Descendants of the Keita met there every seven years to reenact the building of an ancient temple.

reportedly employed magic and witchcraft. Sundiata
defeated the powerful Sosso ruler. The southern chiefdoms gave Sundiata their allegiance, and they became
the core of the new empire of Mali.

Sundiata's victory led to expansion to the north,
and Mali gained control of entry points to the Saharan
trails. At the same time, Sundiata's army extended Mali
to the west over Senegal's upper valley, toward the
Gambia. Mali now controlled internal trade routes,
making it possible for gold to be transported north to
meet the Saharan trade.

Camels were the new carriers across the desert.
Traders from the Sudan brought gold to the Sahel, an
area stretching across Africa from the Atlantic Ocean
in the west to the Red Sea in the east, and exchanged
it for salt brought there by the nomadic Berbers from
mines in the Sahara. (Sahel means "shore" in Arabic.)
Towns along the way developed as ports. By the eighth
and ninth centuries, most of the traders traveling the
Sahara were Muslim. Under Sundiata, Mali came to
rule the Sahel. Mansa Musa inherited these riches and
these lands. Other items that were traded included
kola nuts, livestock, dried fish, shea butter, iron, textiles,
copper, ivory, leatherwork, and slaves. Mansa Musa
profited by imposing import duties on copper, which
was exported throughout the central Sudan region.

SAHARA

Camels became important to the exchange of gold and salt across Africa and the Sahara for traders and nomad intermediaries.

Some historians have noted that without the trade, Mali would not have risen to power and that the first Malian king would not have converted to Islam.

NIANI, MALI'S CAPITAL

After defeating the Sosso people, Sundiata came to Niani, a small ancestral village on the Sankarani River, and made it into his capital. Niani was just one of several Malian capitals that existed over time. Travelers came to Niani. It covered a vast area and was no mere village. Houses built of clay resembled cones with wood and reed roofs. The king's palaces were grouped together and protected by an outer wall. Niani was a stopping place for travelers and caravans from the Maghreb. This area of northern Africa along the Mediterranean Sea included parts of present-day Morocco, Tunisia, Algeria, and Libya. Caravans also arrived from Ifriqiya (present-day Tunisia and eastern Algeria) and Egypt.

CHAPTER TWO

THE GOLDEN AGE OF MANSA MUSA

● ● ● ● ● ● ● ● ● ● ●

Sundiata's record of accomplishments set the stage
for future rulers of Mali. Griots, poets of the time,
built on the strong oral tradition and composed
a long poem of Sundiata in the fourteenth century. This
epic reflects a period of great political and religious
upheaval. It has been shared from one generation to
the next in praise of the ruler who defeated the Sossos
and brought Mali to greatness. Sundiata is sometimes
referred to as Mari Diata the Great.

The poem narrates the story of a prophecy made
to Maghan Kon Fatta, a Malinke ruler in the early thirteenth century. Hunters from a foreign land tell him that
he will have a glorious son, but he must first marry an
ugly woman. Several years pass and Maghan Kon Fatta
is presented with a woman who has a hunched back
and large eyes. Although already married and father of a
healthy son, he remembers the prophecy and takes the
hunchback as a second wife. The son she bears, however,

20

GRIOT (IMPROVISATORE) OF NIANTANSO (TYPE OF MALINKA).

It was the griot's responsibility to safeguard Mali's ancient and oral traditions through poetry and song.

is lame and his head is too large for his body. Still believing in the prophecy, Maghan Kon Fatta names this son, Sundiata, as his heir. But when the king dies, his council ignores his wishes. The son from his first marriage assumes the throne. When Maghan Kon Fatta's second wife believes harm will come to Sundiata, who grows stronger with every day, they leave Mali. Meanwhile, the Sossos overtake Mali. Mali turns to the exiled prince for deliverance from oppression. Sundiata's old playmates have now become the chieftains of Mali. Sundiata defeats the Sossos. King after king pays homage to Sundiata, and the Empire of Mali forms.

The kings of the twelve Mandinka kingdoms lost their legal right to rule. However, Sundiata received their allegiance and appointed them as governors in return. Sundiata reigned over them and the new Empire of Mali for twenty-five years, from 1230 to 1255. He named himself Mansa—king of kings, or emperor.

THE SUCCESSION TO THE THRONE AFTER SUNDIATA

The ability to claim family roots tracing back to Sundiata helped potential rulers ascend to the throne of Mali and establish the Keita family dynasty. Sundiata's son Uli succeeded him on the throne. Mansa Uli was considered a great king, and he made a pilgrimage to Mecca, according to the traditions of Muslim faith. He also conquered the trading centers of Timbuktu and Djenné. He ruled from 1255 to 1270. His brother Wati followed him as ruler and reigned for four years. Then the authority to rule Mali passed to Khalifa, the last of Sundiata's three sons. Khalifa, however, was weak. Devoted to archery, he had a habit of using his bow and arrow to kill people at will. He was considered to be insane, and the people rose up to kill him.

Mansa Uli, Sundiata's son, conquered Djenné, an important center of trade and the site of this mosque.

Sundiata had a daughter, and her son, Abu Bakr, became king even while Khalifa was still technically in power. This shift to a daughter's son, a female line, marked a change in the usual line of royal succession, which was based on patrilineal tradition. Oral narratives have noted that this occurred perhaps because Sundiata had adopted Abu Bakr as his son or perhaps because those who deposed Khalifa wanted someone who had not been in direct line for succession on the throne so they could control him.

Abu Bakr ruled for twelve years. Then a freed slave named Sakura took the throne from him in 1285. Although Sakura had usurped his power, he was deemed to be a great leader with mighty authority and military strength, attracting merchants and the awe of other Sudanese nations. He made his pilgrimage to Mecca but was killed during his return trip in 1300.

The throne reverted to Sundiata's legitimate heirs. Mansa Qu, son of Mansa Uli, reigned and was succeeded by his son, Mansa Mohammad, in 1305. Then the kingship passed back to descendants of Sundiata's siblings.

Family relationships in Malian history were not always clear because records were not written down.

Instead they were passed down from one generation to the next through stories and poems. Mansa Musa was said to be the son of one of Sundiata's brothers, also named Abu Bakr. However, it is more likely, given the years they lived and reigned, that he was Abu Bakr's grandson and Sundiata's grandnephew. Oral histories sometimes deleted generations from the family tree if the people, like Mansa Musa's father, were not considered to be significant.

THE COURT OF MANSA MUSA

The reign of Abu Bakr II, most likely the son of one of Sundiata's sisters, followed the reign of Mansa Mohammad. During his rule, Abu Bakr II sent out an Atlantic expedition with two hundred ships, equipped with men and gold, water, and provisions to last for years. The journey would last until they reached the end of the Atlantic Ocean or until their food and water gave out. Only one ship returned. Abu Bakr II then prepared two thousand ships—one thousand for himself and his men and another one thousand for water and provisions. Before leaving, he named Musa I his successor. Abu Bakr never returned.

THE ARAB STORYTELLERS: IBN BATTUTA

Among the international Silk Road travelers of the fourteenth century were people who kept records of the events they witnessed and the people they met. Much of what is known about Mansa Musa comes from Moroccan traveler Ibn Battuta. As a young man, he set off from his home in Tangier in 1325 for Mecca, according to traditional Muslim custom. His curiosity took him to all corners of the Islamic world, traveling with caravans across the mighty Sahara to North Africa and China. Ten months after leaving Morocco, he arrived in Alexandria, Egypt. He had a dream about a long journey ahead of him, a trek that would take him to many different parts of the world. In Cairo, he wrote about the narrow streets, twelve thousand water carriers, thirty thousand porters, and thirty-six thousand boats on the Nile. He visited Bethlehem and Jerusalem and eventually arrived in the Holy City of Mecca. But instead of returning home, he continued on his travels throughout present-day eastern Russia, Turkey, and China.

Three years after his trip to the East, Ibn Battuta trekked on the back of a camel with a

Moroccan traveler Ibn Battutta recorded the stories he heard about Mansa Musa's pilgrimage to Mecca.

(CONTINUED ON THE NEXT PAGE)

(CONTINUED FROM THE PREVIOUS PAGE)

merchant caravan across the Sahara to Mali. There, in July 1352, he praised the religious practices of the Muslims. He sought out Mansa Musa's grandson, Mansa Sulayman, who now ruled. Stories flowed about Mansa Musa's generosity in Cairo during his pilgrimage to Mecca. Ibn Battuta returned home thirty years later.

Ibn Battuta worked with an Andalusian poet, Ibn Juzayy, to write a book about his travels. Of Mali, he wrote about the sultan's pavilion, his council, the people who were humble servants before their king, and the lack of oppression. He also shared traditional oral stories he had heard from the people. His manuscript, written in Arabic, is in the Bibliothèque Nationale in Paris, France.

Mansa Musa began his reign in 1312. He moved into the palace in Niani, where he presided on a great balcony in a grand seat of ebony, flanked by elephant tusks. The executioner and herald were always at hand. Mansa Musa dictated his orders to his staff. He never spoke directly to his subjects. Instead, a spokesman repeated what he said. No one was allowed into the king's presence wearing sandals, the usual footwear. No one was allowed to sneeze either, and if the king himself sneezed, others beat their hands against their chests.

Everything about Mansa Musa's existence suggested wealth and power. There were displays of gold, silver, and ivory, and a bodyguard of slaves armed with weapons. Saddled and bridled horses stood ready should the king and his entourage need to ride. Two rams protected the palace and the king against the evil eye.

Mansa Musa wore a long robe made of European cloth. His trousers were made of twenty pieces of cloth. No other man could wear such pants. However, when a hero returned from his exploits, Mansa Musa gave him a wide pair of trousers. The ruler also wore a turban with one end dangling in his face.

He had a large harem that included beautiful girls from all over his country. He had more than one wife. The first wife was known as the senior wife. Mansa Musa's senior wife was Inari Kunate, who accompanied him on his later pilgrimage to Mecca.

The king of Mali employed scribes, although his orders were mostly given orally. Correspondence was used mostly to establish and maintain relations outside Mali. For example, Mansa Musa sent a book written by one of his scribes to the sultan of Egypt.

The man closest to Mansa Musa was the head of his slaves. Slaves, especially those born in captivity, were considered to be fiercely loyal. The most prominent court official was the *dyeli*, who also served as the griot and spokesman. The dyeli had the responsibility of being the custodian of the all-important oral tradition. Every prince had his own dyeli to remind him of his ancestry and his obligations. The dyeli proved to be the king's best friend and confidant. He also became the master of ceremonies at festivals. In a caste-based system, the dyeli were considered to be of low status. This status, their reliance on the king, and the fact that they had no relatives among the nobility or free men made them good choices for such access and proximity to the emperor of Mali.

Ibn Batutta related an anecdote he heard during his travels in Mali. When Mansa Musa was just a boy and without any influence or power, a man gave him seven *mithqals*, gold coins used as currency in the early Islamic world and in parts of Africa. This man later came to Mansa Musa when he was emperor of Mali to settle a dispute. Mansa Musa recognized him and had him sit next to him on his throne. He got the man to admit the kindness he had shown years before and asked his commanders how he should reward such a good deed. They said the ruler

BY ANY OTHER NAME

Mansa Musa preferred to be known as the lord of Mali. However, Egyptians referred to him as the king of Takrur (part of Senegal). Mansa Musa objected to this title. Takrur, he said, was only one of his states. He was also sometimes called Gongo or Kanku Musa, son of the woman Gongo/Kanku, his mother's name. It had been the custom in the Keita family to distinguish members with common names by adding the first name of the mother. Other names used to refer to Mansa Musa included the Lion of Mali, Lord of the Mines of Wangara, Emir of Melle, and Conqueror of Ghanata.

should give the man ten times the amount originally given. But to Mansa Musa, that was not enough. He rewarded the man with seven hundred mithqals, a robe of honor, and male and female slaves. He ordered the man not to cut himself off from contact with him.

Mansa Musa was the most important of black Muslim kings of western Africa. He commanded the largest and most powerful army. His subjects respected him, and his enemies feared him.

A NEW GOLD STANDARD FOR SALT

There could be no doubt that Mansa Musa's empire had wealth. Its source was its gold and salt mines. At the time of the Empire of Ghana, the location of gold mines was a closely guarded secret. Gold was required for other lands to make their coinage. In the thirteenth century, demand increased for gold throughout Europe when its countries returned to the gold standard and raised the value. This demand peaked during Mansa Musa's reign. Additionally, gold continued to be used for coins, jewelry, weapons, and various other symbols of wealth and status throughout western Africa.

Salt was necessary to counteract the loss of the body's salt through perspiration in the Sudan. People far inland in the Sudan exchanged gold for salt on an ounce-for-ounce basis.

Prosperity, land, power, and dedication to Islamic art and culture made Mansa Musa's time on the throne the golden age of the Mali Empire. Mansa

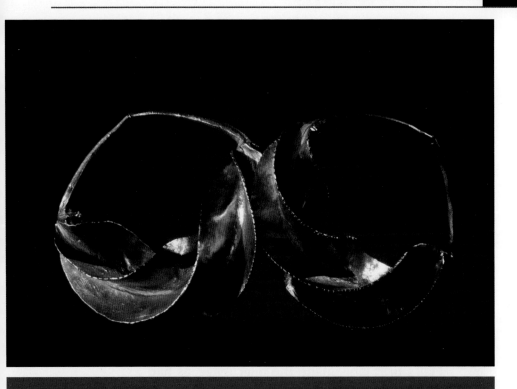

The availability of gold made it popular in fourteenth-century Mali. Women wore earrings made from this gold.

Musa claimed it would take four months to travel from one end of his kingdom lengthwise and at least as long in width. The exact size of his empire at its peak remains unclear, but it is certain that the cultural impact of his rule reached even farther. At the time of his death, the empire extended from the borders of Takrur in the west to Dendi in the east and from Walata, Arawan, and Tadmekket in the Sahara to Futa Jallon in the south.

CHAPTER THREE

TIME FOR A PILGRIMAGE

● ● ● ● ● ● ● ● ● ● ●

People of the Islamic faith learn early the importance of making a pilgrimage to Mecca, the birthplace of the prophet Muhammad. Mansa Musa's family was no different. Barmandana, Mali's first king, made the pilgrimage, as had Sundiata's son Mansa Uli, and Sakura the usurper. In the first year of his reign as the emperor of Mali, Mansa Musa stipulated that Islam be Mali's official religion. He fostered the growth of Islam throughout the empire.

The Islamic faith connected Mali with other Muslim nations. Versions such as this of the Quran, the holy book of Islam, began appearing around northern and western Africa.

FOLLOWING THE LAWS OF ISLAM

As a follower of Islam, Mansa Musa gained entry to the culture and kingdoms of the eastern Mediterranean, which would ease his relationships and his travels. As Mali expanded into the Sahel, old Islamic centers such as Dia and Walata became part of the empire. Muslim traders operated through an ever-widening network of trade routes in Mali, and these traders, in addition to northern African Muslims, came to live in Mali's capital. From Sundiata's time, Mali grew from a small Malinke chiefdom into a vast, multiethnic empire, now with great Muslim influence inside and extensive Islamic relations outside. As with the trade routes, Islam contributed to the nation's unity. Mansa Musa was not a god-hero like Sundiata. He was a pious and righteous Muslim. He built mosques, many of which had minarets, and instituted Friday prayer, the public prayer, and the call to prayer, according to the five Pillars of Islam.

Despite his own faith, Mansa Musa knew not to force his subjects to convert to Islam. Many in Mansa Musa's realm still believed in spirits and magic. Even the *Epic of Sundiata* referred to the hero as a magician. Musa had determined that the gold mines were better kept in the hands of the pagans. Tribute paid to him for the gold was

FIVE PILLARS OF ISLAM

Followers of Islam worship God, or Allah, directly without priests, clergy, or saints. The believer has duties, however, and they are named in the five Pillars of Islam: belief, worship, fasting, almsgiving, and pilgrimage.

- Belief: The believer must testify in Arabic that "there is no god but God and that Muhammad is his messenger." This profession of faith, or *shahada*, is central to Islam because it affirms God as a single deity and it affirms the role of Muhammad as prophet. The shahada is used in calls to prayer and also appears on flags and coins.
- Worship: The follower worships God five times a day: at dawn, noon, mid-afternoon, sunset, and nightfall. To properly worship requires ritual washing, prostrating on the ground in the direction of Mecca, and reciting certain phrases. Men traditionally gather on Friday for the noon prayer and listen to a

sermon in Arabic. In many places women may also attend, but they must remain segregated from the men.

- Fasting: Believers must refrain from drinking, eating, smoking, and intimate relations between sunrise and sunset during Ramadan, the ninth month according to the Muslim calendar. A feast to break the fast takes place at the end of the month.
- Almsgiving: Muslims must give alms to the poor. They are to donate a fixed amount of money to charity every year. Muslims can also be taxed on certain possessions in order to provide for the poor.
- Pilgrimage: Followers of Islam must undertake a pilgrimage, or *hajj*, to Mecca at least once in their lifetimes, preferably during the first days of the twelfth month in the Muslim calendar. Once in Mecca, the pilgrim wears a special garment of white cloth. Those who complete the pilgrimage earn the title of *hajji*, one who has made pilgrimage, a title of great respect.

essential to his country's economy. Mali did not govern the gold mines directly, but it did own the trade routes. Mansa Musa had to strike a truce with the pagans to ensure duties were paid to him. The king of Mali noticed that whenever a gold province was conquered and Islam filtered in, gold production there ceased while output in neighboring regions increased. Only through the pagan ritual practice of associating with the local spirits did it seem that the land produced the precious metal.

A CARAVAN LIKE NO OTHER

Mansa Musa had to travel to perform the duties of a Muslim. He had to adhere to all five Pillars of Islam, the fifth being the hajj, or pilgrimage, to Mecca. The journey would take more than one year. Crossing the Sinai Desert from Egypt alone would take two months. He would have to travel some 9,000 miles (14,484 km). But he had another mission as well. He wanted to recruit teachers and leaders. He also yearned to learn more about the Prophet's teachings. One account of his preparations maintained that Musa had accidentally killed his mother, Nana Gongo. In agony, he donated a large sum of money to charity. He resolved to fast. He asked a Muslim scholar

Followers of Islam are expected to make a pilgrimage to Mecca at least once in their lifetime. Mansa Musa could have been among pilgrims like these.

who specialized in sacred law for advice. The advisor told him to seek sanctuary with the Prophet and ask him to intervene on his behalf with Allah. According to this story, Mansa Musa vowed to make pilgrimage that same day.

Mansa Musa called for the collection of provisions from all over Mali. He asked for guidance on choosing the most appropriate day for setting out. He would need, he was told, to wait for a Saturday on the twelfth day of a month. He had to wait nine months for such a day.

The journey required traveling over several types of terrain. Traveling across the Sahara would be dangerous. Surrounded by such a large entourage, Mansa Musa had little to fear. But other Muslims making the journey were not as fortunate and did not have as much protection and so many assets at their disposal. Attacks by Bedouins, or northern African nomads, were known to happen frequently. There were also jungles to contend with. It could take a typical pilgrim years to arrive in Mecca. A poor man might stop along the way to work and earn his way. Some pilgrims were taken captive and forced into slavery. Traveling with a caravan offered safety. Caravans might have had as many as six thousand people traveling together.

Traveling in caravans like this shielded people from potential harm. Thousands could travel together at one time.

Such a caravan paled against Mansa Musa's preparations. Other Mali kings had made the hajj before him, but perhaps without as much fanfare. His entourage included sixty thousand people, twelve thousand of whom were personal servants dressed in brocade and silk from Yemen. Eighty camels carried 24,000 pounds (10,886 kilograms) of precious gold. Each camel carried 300 pounds (136 kg). In Mali, only slave men and women would carry the gold. But when traveling long distances, animals were used, too. Hundreds of horses were part of the caravan. Slaves carried the provisions. Eight thousand soldiers from Mansa Musa's army of one hundred thousand came along to guard the caravan. State dignitaries accompanied him, too. Five hundred slaves were prepared to step before their king. Each carried a gold staff weighing 4 pounds (2 kg). Mansa Musa's caravan was a large, moving city.

With such an imposing array of resources, Mansa Musa may well have also had in mind cementing cultural, political, and economic relationships with important Muslim centers in the Islamic world. If anyone could carry out such a mission, he could. His faith and his gold would help to open doors. He named his son Muhammad as deputy during his absence. Faith would guide him safely through the desert. It was his duty to make the pilgrimage.

He put his right foot into the saddle and mounted his black stallion. He gave the signal. The red and yellow flags unfurled. Slowly the huge caravan began to move.

Mansa Musa was ready for the greatest adventure of his life.

CHAPTER FOUR

NINE THOUSAND MILES

• • • • • • • • • • • •

M ansa Musa and his great caravan moved out
from the capital city of Niani and traveled
along the Niger River to Mema, taking a
northeasterly route to Egypt. Through the grasslands they trekked with sights of herds of giraffes,
elephants, and gazelles. In Mali, even sheep and goats
had no place to graze, but now Mansa Musa and his
people could see the vast open spaces. They came
to Walata, on the southern edge of the Sahara. The
heat there was staggering. It had mud brick houses,
barren hills, and just a few palm trees. They had then
traveled more than 500 miles (800 km) through
sand to Taghaza, a desolate place but one where
gold was exchanged freely. Before the caravan lay an
unimaginable expanse of desert. It was best to travel
in the early morning and late afternoon to avoid the

Walata, shown here in present-day Mauritania, was one of Mansa Musa's first stops on his pilgrimage to Mecca.

terrible heat. They rested under awnings. They drank precious water from goatskin bags. Despite the precautions and provisions, the caravan still suffered during the long, hard journey across the unforgiving desert. Throughout the trip, Mansa Musa freely gave presents and alms to tribes he encountered.

THROUGH THE GRASSLAND AND ACROSS THE DESERT

Mansa Musa's pilgrimage across the Sahara proved that by the fourteenth century, the desert could indeed be safely crossed, at least by a powerful king with an enormous body of followers. It showed that western African lands had formed mighty states and that their peoples—at least some of them—had become pious Muslims.

Traveling across the Sahara was important to the gold trade, of course, between the Sudan and the Islamic world and Christian Europe. The pilgrimage also represented the great age of camel caravans across the Sahara, which lasted for more than a millennium. Even as the desert's global role in the world's economy decreased between 1500 and 1900, routes through its vast sands led to increased commerce and political, social, and cultural developments within Africa.

The Sahara covers 3.6 million square miles (9.3 million square km). Mansa Musa's pilgrimage entered the Sahara at a southwestern point, but not at its westernmost edge.

THE GREAT CARAVAN ARRIVES IN CAIRO

After eight months, the caravan eventually reached Egypt and camped near the pyramids for three days. Mansa Musa sent a gift of fifty thousand dinars to the sultan of Egypt, Al-Malik al-Nasir, announcing his arrival. The amount of the gift clearly signaled the Malian emperor's greatness. He entered Cairo in July 1324 and remained for three months before continuing his pilgrimage to the sacred city of Mecca.

In his own realm, Mansa Musa was used to his subjects bearing a crown of dust or ash upon their heads and groveling before him. Here in Egypt, however, the great ruler was required to kiss the ground before the Egyptian sultan. However, Mansa Musa controlled more land and more resources than the sultan of Egypt. He would not grovel before him. He declined the invitation to visit with the sultan. His mission was only to make pilgrimage, he said. But eventually he gave in and agreed to meet with the Egyptian ruler. Rather than prostrate himself to the sultan, he did so in the name of Allah. This act demonstrated his Muslim faith and respect for the sultan. The sultan half-rose to meet him and they sat side by side as equals. Their conversation lasted a long time.

The Citadel of Cairo served as the seat of power of Egyptian sultans, including Al-Malik al-Nasir. As great a city as Cairo was, Mansa Musa controlled more land and more resources.

Although Mansa Musa spoke perfect Arabic, he communicated to the public only through his interpreter, much as he did at his own court.

The sultan showed the Malian emperor the respect and treatment his position deserved. He lent him a palace for his stay in Cairo. He presented Mansa Musa and his officers robes of honor. The robe for the emperor was an Alexandrian open-fronted cloak trimmed in fur and gold thread and held by gold fastenings. He was given a silken skullcap with Islamic emblems, a gold inlaid belt, a sword, an embroidered ker-chief with pure gold, and two horses saddled and bridled. The sultan of Egypt also ordered provisions for the remainder of Mansa Musa's trip to Mecca. Before he had left Niani, Mansa Musa wanted to learn more about Islamic sacred law. In Cairo, he learned that even a king could not take four wives according to the laws of Islam.

Mansa Musa distributed his gold widely as a show of his wealth and generosity. He gave out so much gold that its value decreased between 10 and 25 percent.

The merchants of Cairo took advantage of the caravan's naïveté and Mansa Musa's generous nature. They sold a shirt, cloak, or robe for five dinars when each actually cost one. The merchants took pride in their ability to deceive the simple people of Mali. But the deceit did not go unnoticed, and the Malian travelers formed a low opinion of Egyptians that outlasted Mansa Musa's reign. Even if a learned doctor were to come to them, once he announced he was Egyptian, the people of Mali would treat him with rudeness.

THE PILGRIMAGE CONTINUES

As October neared, it was time to continue on to Mecca. The people of Cairo would not soon forget Mansa Musa. As in the first leg of his pilgrimage, he

GOLD AND THE ECONOMY

Mansa Musa had the power to single-handedly control the gold market. Several Arabic writers described his visit to Cairo and how his distribution of gold affected the economy. When the Malian emperor first arrived, the price of gold was high. According to the historian al-Umari, Mansa Musa depleted his gold in Mecca and returned to Cairo empty-handed. There he had to borrow

Cairo's merchants consistently overcharged the people of Mali for their wares in bazaars like this one,.

(CONTINUED ON THE NEXT PAGE)

(CONTINUED FROM THE PREVIOUS PAGE)

money and pledged his credit to the merchants at high interest rates. The merchants made seven hundred dinars profit on three hundred. Al-Umari collected his information from the people of Cairo, who were eager to recount what they had seen of the Malian emperor's opulent spending. Al-Umari reported that the value of gold remained low for twelve years. Mansa Musa eventually paid back all his debts.

While the price of gold fell with long-lasting results, the news of Mansa Musa's open display of wealth traveled far and wide to other parts of the world. He was a force to be reckoned with and deserved worldwide attention. Even in 2012, he was named the richest man who had ever lived, with a worth of $400 billion by today's standards.

was dressed splendidly. His reputation for generosity and opulence continued. With ample provisions and baggage and riding camels from the sultan, Mansa Musa and his caravan crossed the Red Sea, eventually reaching what is now Saudi Arabia's western coast. The sultan of Egypt had arranged for feeding stations for the caravan's animals, and he had given the Egyptian commanders of the pilgrimage a written order to look after and respect the emperor of Mali.

IN THE HOLY CITY OF MECCA

Mansa Musa's caravan finally arrived in Mecca. As a follower of Islam, Mansa Musa had to adhere to the rites of the pilgrimage once he reached the birthplace of the prophet Muhammad. Each stage of the pilgrimage involved a ritual from which the pilgrim could not deviate. The high point of the pilgrimage was a visit to Arafat, the hill from which the Prophet delivered his Farewell Sermon to those who had completed the hajj with him.

For twelve days, Mansa Musa followed the rituals. He wore a plain, seamless white garment. He wore no jewelry or other decorations. He no longer appeared as the mighty ruler he was. He was a Muslim who had come to Mecca, like so many other devoted followers. One ritual is to enter the Great Mosque, circle the ancient stone building at its center seven times, each time kissing

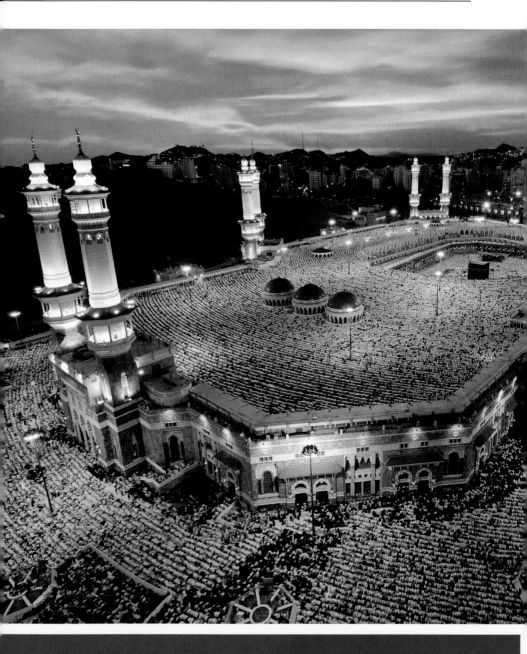

The Great Mosque in Mecca was and still is a central site for performing pilgrimage rituals according to the laws of Islam.

or touching the sacred Black Stone, and pray. He then moved on to the Station of Abraham and prostrated himself there twice. He would follow this with a drink of water at Zamzam, the well bestowed by God. Mansa Musa crossed to the hills of al-Safa and al-Marwah, symbols of patience and perseverance. After reciting specific prayers, he walked seven times between the two hills. This completed the rituals at the Sacred House.

Mansa Musa stayed three months in Mecca. He requested that two or three descendants of the Prophet accompany him back to Mali. He wanted his subjects to be blessed by them. At first, the request was denied. The grand sharif of Mecca did not want to place these holy men in harm's way should infidels attack the caravan. Mansa Musa continued to make his plea, and the sharif agreed that any descendants could go with the Malian emperor should they wish to. Mansa Musa announced in the mosques that he would give a thousand mithqals of gold to any of the Prophet's descendants to accompany him back to Mali. Four men from the Prophet's tribe accepted his offer. They, along with their families, joined the king's entourage.

Many other people accompanied Mansa Musa home. They included Egyptian merchants, Quran scholars, and the holy men from the Prophet's tribe. In Mecca, he met the celebrated Granada poet and architect Abu-Ishaq Ibrahim-es-Saheli. The ruler persuaded him to join him on his return to Mali. Mansa Musa also brought home books.

Mansa Musa had now earned the title of hajji, one who had made the pilgrimage.

CHAPTER FIVE

OFF TO TIMBUKTU

• • • • • • • • • • • •

Mansa Musa had spent all his money by the time he returned to Cairo from Mecca. He needed money, and he borrowed from a man named Siraj al-Din. Mansa Musa had stayed in his gardens outside Cairo when he first stopped on his way to Mecca. Siraj al-Din wanted to be sure he would get his money back, so he sent an agent with the caravan to claim the money. But the agent decided to stay in Mali. Siraj al-Din decided to travel to Mali himself and demand his repayment. He brought his son with him. When they arrived at Timbuktu, es-Saheli served as his host. Siraj al-Din died that night, and people suspected that he had been poisoned. But the son spoke up and said he had eaten the very same food and he was fine. The son arrived in Mali, claimed his money, and returned to Egypt. Mansa Musa had been true to his word.

THE ARAB STORYTELLERS: IBN KHALDUN AND AL-UMARI

Ibn Battuta was just one of several Arab storytellers who were instrumental in spreading the name of Mansa Musa and stories about his travels. Ibn Khaldun was a well-known Arab historian. Born in Tunisia in 1332, he spent most of his life in the service of northern African rulers. He wrote of diplomatic exchanges between Mali and Morocco. Like Ibn Battuta, he, too, learned about Mansa Musa from local men and told their stories in his writings. Ibn Khaldun also wrote about the kings who preceded Mansa Musa, and he was the source of information about the work of Andalusian architect es-Saheli.

Another Arabic scholar, Shihab ad-Din Ahmad ibn Fadl Allah al-Umari, known as al-Umari, was born in Damascus in 1301. He was interested in collecting and recording stories, and travel served this purpose. He visited Cairo years after Mansa Musa's pilgrimage. He found officials and others still talking about the Malian king's time there, especially his gifts and purchases in gold. He also interviewed people who had lived in Mali for many years and were able to describe the court at Mali. Al-Umari died in Damascus in 1349. His complete work, called *Pathways of Vision in the Realms of the Metropolises*, has never been published.

Arab storyteller Ibn Khaldun told the stories of Mansa Musa's architect, es-Saheli.

GOOD NEWS ARRIVES

While traveling across the desert, news reached Mansa Musa that one of his generals, Sagmandia, captured Gao, the capital of the Songhay people. In the ninth century, Gao was one of western Africa's most important trading centers. It was also a powerful kingdom. Within it were subservient kingdoms that gave the king of Gao their allegiance. It was considered a port along the trans-Saharan trade route. It established trade relations with Algeria. Gao had once before been conquered by the Malian king Sakura in the thirteenth century.

The Songhay kingdom had been known as early as the seventh century. It occupied the areas around the great bend of the Niger River. Like Malians, the Songhays traded in salt and gold through Gao, Djenné, and Timbuktu. But now Gao belonged to Mali.

The kingdom of Gao measured 1,000 miles (1,609 km) across and was quite a coup for Mali. It meant an enormous geographic extension of the Empire of Mali. It also meant rich copper fields now belonged to Mali. Mansa Musa, overjoyed at the news, decided to delay his return to Niani by visiting Gao. He wanted to inspect his newly acquired city and pay his respects to the dethroned king. He took a different route

The Songhay city of Gao became the property of Mansa Musa and Mali. In Gao lies the tomb of sixteenth-century Songhay ruler Askia Mohammed.

this time to travel west. He stopped at Ghadames, once the site of an ancient Roman fort (and now in present-day Libya). There he met a man who conducted guerilla raids and wanted Mansa Musa's help against his enemy, the ruler of Wargala. He asked for this assistance based on the emperor of Mali's highly regarded and dreaded power in the desert. It is not known whether Mansa Musa honored this request, but the man joined the caravan to Mali.

In Gao, the emperor of the state of Songhay greeted him and gave up his two sons as hostages. Songhay was yet no match for the mighty Mali Empire. But as Mali's power began to decline after Mansa Musa's death, Songhay stood ready to reclaim its land and assume a new authority.

ALL THE WAY TO TIMBUKTU

Mansa Musa's army also conquered the Songhay city of Timbuktu. From Gao, the emperor continued his journey home and made Timbuktu his next stop. Timbuktu was the second most important Songhay town. It had been founded by the Tuareg peoples around 1100 CE. It grew into an important trade center, and Mansa Musa developed it even more as a commercial city,

The Sankore Mosque in Timbuktu was the brainchild of Mansa Musa and es-Saheli. It laid the foundation for learning across the empire.

where caravans could make connections with northern African centers such as Egypt, Ghadames, Fez, Tuat, and other places. But commercial activity was not the only development on his mind. He envisioned Timbuktu as a center of culture and learning. Already scholars there were skilled theologians, well versed in Islamic law. With es-Saheli's help, the mosque of Sankore arose as a center of instruction and laid the foundation for the University of Sankore. The university would serve not only Africa, but also the entire Middle East. Es-Saheli encouraged Mansa Musa to bring learned Muslim scholars to

ES-SAHELI BUILT IT AND THEY CAME

Abu-Ishaq Ibrahim-es-Saheli was already a well-known poet and architect when he met Mansa Musa in Mecca in 1324. He was born in Granada in the Moorish-ruled province of Andalusia in Spain. He came from a trustworthy family of wealth. His father had been head of the perfumers' guild. Es-Saheli learned law and worked as a public officer to authorize documents. He left Granada for Cairo and made his pilgrimage to Mecca. His magnificent skill remains in view today with the Djinguereber Mosque in Timbuktu in Mali. The structure requires little maintenance, although its existence has been threatened by armed terrorist groups. The mosque was named a UNESCO World Heritage Site in 1988 and was later listed as an endangered site in 2013 following an attack.

Es-Saheli, who took on the name al-Tuwayjin, settled in Timbuktu and become known as a celebrated scholar. He traveled to Fez (in present-day Morocco) as an ambassador for Mansa Musa. They had decided to send Sudanese scholars to Fez for study. He died in 1346. He is credited with introducing a unique Sudanese style of architecture.

Timbuktu to build schools and the university.

Timbuktu stood at the crossroads of Ghana and Songhay, about 4 miles (6.4 km) from the Niger River. It took on the mantel of being the entry point to the Sahara and Saharan trade. It remained under Mali's rule until the fifteenth century.

These unplanned visits to Gao and Timbuktu inspired Mansa Musa. He commissioned es-Saheli to build mosques in both cities. In Gao, the mosque was made of burnt brick and continued to be a source of admiration into the seventeenth century. Such a structure reinforced Mali's power in this conquered land. But the mosque in Timbuktu became Mansa Musa's pride and joy. Called the Djinguereber Mosque, it was built in 1327. Es-Saheli showed his European background. His use of protruding beams recalled the use of buttresses in Europe and allowed workers to continue to add mud to the building. Timbuktu's rainy season made this permanent scaffolding necessary to maintain the building. The mosque's two minarets reminded people of the pyramids of Egypt. Two thousand people could pray simultaneously in this magnificent structure. It was constructed of mud brick, made by wrapping wet soil around limestone. The mosque featured three

The Djinguereber Mosque in Timbuktu reflects architectural methods es-Saheli learned in Europe, but the style of protruding timbers and mud walls was distinctly his.

inner courts and twenty-five rows of pillars aligned in an east-west direction.

Es-Saheli received forty thousand mithqals of gold for this work. In Timbuktu, he also built a palace, Madugu. Timbuktu was no longer a rough place for trading. It had become the center of Islamic learning and an important business link to Europe, the Middle East, and the western African coast.

Mansa Musa's trip had been successful on so many levels. He had made his pilgrimage and followed the rituals required by his faith. He had confirmed trade relations, diplomatic relations, and Islamic connections.

Ready to leave Timbuktu after his long journey, Mansa Musa prepared for the overland trek home to Niani. Meanwhile, he sent the baggage, the women, and the holy men from Mecca home by boat along the Niger.

Mansa Musa could now call himself the great conqueror and the great builder.

CHAPTER SIX

ALL THAT GLITTERS IS MORE THAN GOLD

• • • • • • • • • • • • •

Mansa Musa may have seemed a changed man upon his return to Niani. The experience of pilgrimage may have increased his faith. Yet, he still ruled a land where Islam stood in conflict with the pagan practices of many of his people who still believed in magic.

For example, the typical Malian practice of throwing dead bodies in the bushes differed drastically from the Islamic practice of burial. Mansa Musa brought back many Arabic scholars and architects to spread Islamic culture and learning. Within his extensive empire, there were four hundred cities and centers of urban living. The region was poised for a time of great change. Mansa Musa had ordinary and extraordinary mosques and minarets built. He established the Friday observances, prayers in congregation, and the call to prayer, according to Islamic custom. Introduction of a

This highly decorative door marks the entry to the fifteenth-century Sidi Yahya mosque in Timbuktu. Such mosques called Muslim followers to prayer.

new style of architecture could distinguish his kingdom even more than gold—and it could last longer.

A NEW STYLE OF ARCHITECTURE

Mansa Musa wanted a house as the seat of his authority. It had to be solidly constructed, and he wanted
it plastered, so the building would stand out among
others. No one had used plaster in this region of Africa
before. Es-Saheli understood his needs perfectly. He
built the emperor a new Hall of Audience, a square
building with a dome. It connected through an inte-
rior door with the royal palace. With knowledge of
handicrafts, he put his skills to the test. He plastered
the structure repeatedly with colored patterns to add
to its elegance. Wood plating adorned the windows
on two floors. Silver foil framed the windows on the
upper floor while gold framed the windows on the
lower floor. Upon seeing this new building, Mansa Musa
was astonished. Es-Saheli demonstrated what a real
architect could do. It shamed the ruler to think about
how ignorant Malian builders had been. He rewarded
es-Saheli with twelve thousand mithqals of gold dust
and continued to shower him with gifts and his favor.

WHAT REMAINS OF MANSA MUSA'S BUILDINGS

Mansa Musa's building program is still evident today throughout Mali. The Djinguereber Mosque continues to astound the world with its unique protruding timbers and walls made from the earth on which it stands. The University of Sankore (also known as the University of Timbuktu) remains and is situated inside the Sankore Mosque. The Gao Mosque also remains. Although the mosques still stand, they do require routine maintenance. The Sankore Mosque required rebuilding.

Unfortunately, the Hall of Audience no longer stands. No structure that Mansa Musa may have ordered built in Niani stands today. In fact, Niani is only a village. There are no artifacts that give evidence of its former role as a royal capital.

Since Gao and Timbuktu are Malian cities today, the mosques stand as a testament to Mansa Musa's vision and es-Saheli's talent. They remind the world of the richest empire that once was and its ruler's desire to create greatness not only for himself, but also for his people and his faith.

EVERYDAY LIFE IN THE MALI EMPIRE

Day-to-day life in Mali continued as it always had. The people of Mali drank water from the river that surrounded Niani on all four sides, or they drank from wells. The area was extremely hot. Wild trees covered the hills. Al-Umari wrote of one tree that gave shade to five hundred horsemen.

The people of Mali ate mostly rice and seeds that resembled mustard seeds. Though wheat was rare, it provided nutrition to them and their animals. They grew cowpeas, gourds, turnips, onions, garlic, eggplant, and cabbage. Fig trees grew everywhere.

Malians used a fat to whitewash their mud homes, light torches and lanterns, and make soap. But this fat could also be eaten if prepared properly and could only be carried in gourds. Its preparation was known to burn down a house or two and would burn through a leather skin bag. Many Malians ate fruits that seemed sour to people who came to Mali from elsewhere.

CONTRIBUTING TO THE ECONOMY

In Mali's savanna region, which could sustain vegetation despite the dry climate, rainfall made agriculture productive. Farmers grew millet, sorghum, and rice. Slaves were settled in new villages to till the land and to fill the emperor's granaries. Any surplus went into the trading network.

Artisans trained in working with iron, hide, and wood also produced saleable goods. These workers belonged to a certain caste. But weavers of textiles were not restricted to this caste. Places such as Timbuktu and Djenné were home to workshops of many weavers and tailors, and these workers belonged to the Muslim elite class.

Conquering Timbuktu gave Mansa Musa the opportunity to create a major city for trade, artisanship, learning, and culture.

Other occupations included fishing and cattle breeding. This diversity of products helped to develop the robust trade within the reaches of Mali as well as beyond it.

PRACTICING ISLAM AT HOME

As a result of Mansa Musa's efforts to spread Islam and Islamic learning in western Africa, the religion began to take a greater hold among ordinary citizens. In Mali, it was each man's practice to send a servant with his prayer mat to the Friday mosque and spread it out for him. These prayer carpets were made from fronds from a tree that resembled the palm tree. It was necessary for the servant to go in advance because otherwise the man might not find a place to pray.

A man with a dirty shirt would wash it for wear at Friday prayer. The men tried to memorize the Quran. They sometimes tied up their children until they knew the Quran by heart, too.

However, although Islam was gaining a wider audience, it did not replace traditional beliefs and practices entirely. Many Malians observed elements of both faiths. Even Mali's rulers likely retained traditional practices.

THE WOMEN OF MALI

Despite the adoption of Islam in Mali, Malian women tended not to wear the traditional veils. It was also a custom that if someone raised a beautiful daughter, he should offer her to the king as a slave to do with her as he wished without the benefit of marriage. When Mansa Musa learned that such a practice was against Islamic law, according to the writings of al-Umari, he vowed to abandon the practice.

Ibn Battuta also wrote of the females of Mali. It disturbed him that servants, slave girls, and little girls appeared naked before men. At festivals, they wore nothing but a sprinkling of dust and ashes on their heads, a way of greeting the king in humility. He noted that during Ramadan when it was the custom to celebrate the breaking of the fast at the house of the sultan, about two hundred slave girls brought out the food, each completely naked. The emperor's daughters went without clothes as well.

A NEW SHELL GAME

While Mansa Musa was known for gold, his kingdom also used cowries, shells from the Indian Ocean, as

Cowries formed an important part of Mali's economy across its vast lands. These shells were used as money.

currency. Since the eleventh century, countries of the western Sudan had been importing these shells. Al-Umari noted their use in Mali, and Ibn Battuta, too, wrote of their use in Gao for buying and selling goods. The use of cowries helped Mali establish an economy across its vast holdings. Gold was used primarily for large transactions and long-distance trade.

THE ANIMALS OF MALI

Animals were a significant part of the Malian landscape. Some threatened humans, while others were threatened by humans. Hunters often sought out wild buffalo in the desert plains. Men would steal away the calves in order to use them to lure the buffalo. The men used bows and poisoned arrows to kill the animals. They ate the meat once the poisoned area of the flesh was removed. Other desert animals included donkeys, cows, gazelles, ostriches, elephants, lions, and panthers. They were not viewed as dangerous unless provoked.

Other animals were found closer to home. Sheep and goats found their food in garbage heaps. Crocodiles swam in the river. A crocodile's gall bladder was considered poisonous but precious and was taken for the king's treasury.

CHAPTER SEVEN

A LEGACY BUILDS

• • • • • • • • • • • •

Upon his return, Mansa Musa intended to hand over his throne to his son. He wanted to return to Mecca and remain there to live a simple and pious life. He was willing to relinquish his wealth to follow his faith. His empire and subjects seemed to be thriving, but in his eyes, there was still work to do to bring his kingdom to even greater heights.

NEW TRADE AND DIPLOMATIC RELATIONS

Trade opportunities opened with Portugal and Italy as they vied with Egypt and the Islamic nations of northern Africa to conduct business with Mali, the wealthiest nation on earth. The relationship with Portugal led later to exploration efforts of the

The mighty Abu al-Hasan, ruler of the Moors of northern Africa and Spain, preferred to associate with other mighty rulers, one of whom was Mansa Musa of Mali.

western African coast to tap into the gold mines
that were there.

Mansa Musa also established diplomatic relations
with the sultans of Morocco. In 1337, he initiated com-
munications with Abu al-Hasan, the conqueror of the
kingdoms of the central Maghreb, by sending off two of
his subjects with an interpreter. Abu al-Hasan already
had a reputation for associating himself with only the
mightiest monarchs. He knew that Musa was the greatest of the Sudanese rulers and accepted Mansa Musa's
initiative. He treated the Malian men with respect and
sent gifts back with them for their emperor. Sadly, Mansa
Musa did not live long enough to see the return of his
subjects or the gifts from Morocco.

The cause of Mansa Musa's death is unknown, but
by the time he died, most likely by 1337, the empire
had reached its maximum size. Its authority stretched
through present-day Mali and parts of Senegal,
Mauritania, Gambia, Guinea, Burkina Faso, and Niger.

Mansa Musa, with the help of es-Saheli and the scholars who accompanied him on his journey back from
Mecca, aimed to introduce Malian centers of culture
and learning to the world. The pilgrimage gave him and
Mali great publicity. News of this great, wealthy king
reached Europe from Egypt and northern Africa.

Abraham Cresques's map, also known as the Catalan map, used gold paint, appropriately, to depict Mansa Musa's crown, orb, and scepter.

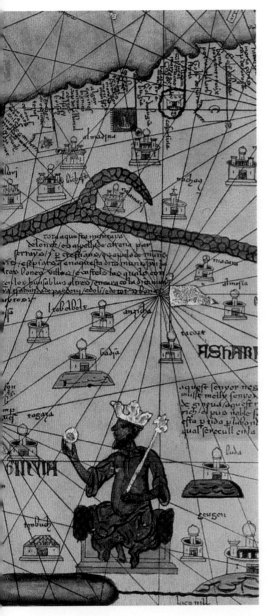

"Rex Melly," the king of Mali, even appeared on a map drawn by Angelino Dulcert in 1339. He also appeared as Mussa Melli on a Spanish map drawn for King Charles V of France by Abraham Cresques of Majorca around the year 1375. Unfortunately, his appearance on these maps came too late for him personally to benefit.

SUCCESSION TO THE THRONE

As expected, the reign of Mali passed to Mansa Musa's son, Muhammad, also known as Mansa Magha. Magha ruled for only

THE CRESQUES MAP

Abraham Cresques came from a Jewish family in Catalonia, Spain, who worked in Majorca in the late fourteenth century. Catalonia was known for its great chart makers, and King Charles V of France commissioned Cresques through one of Cresques's patrons. The project was a large one. Cresques was to complete an atlas of the world. It was a *mappa mundi*, which meant it was to provide an image of the world, its regions, and its peoples. The final *Catalan Atlas* consisted of twelve pages. Four showed cosmic and astrological information. The remaining eight sheets formed the map itself. Cresques paid particular attention to the East and to Africa. He illustrated the map with the image of Mansa Musa of Mali. He used gold leaf to paint Mansa Musa's crown and scepter and showed him holding a golden disc. Other figures depicted include Alexander the Great, Kublai Khan, and the Marco Polo caravan crossing the Silk Road. The atlas is now housed at the Bibliothèque Nationale in Paris.

four years; it was rumored his time as king was cut short by his uncle, Mansa Musa's brother, Sulayman.

It was now to Sulayman that Abu al-Hasan sent presents. But by this time, Mali had become a troubled empire. Sulayman threw a lavish reception for the members of the Moroccan embassy and honored them throughout their visit in Mali. The Moroccans returned to their own land, accompanied by Malian dignitaries, who praised the Moroccan sultan. They talked of Sulayman paying duties to the sultan and of his submission to his authority. The sultan was now satisfied that he had risen above other kings. But this act could have been a shrewd move by Mansa Sulayman to gain the sultan's support. This support, however, was short-lived.

Mansa Sulayman and his emissaries witnessed the revolt of the people of Morocco against Abu al-Hasan, and they narrowly escaped with their lives. Abu al-Hasan was beaten, his ships sunk, and his son seized what remained of his kingdom. Abu al-Hasan's great ambition had worked against him. He died in 1351, and Mansa Sulayman held a memorial service for him in Mali. Diplomatic ties between the two countries withered.

Ibn Battuta visited Mansa Sulayman's court.

Abu al-Hasan is buried on this elaborate site. In the end, he found only defeat, and after his death, diplomatic relations with Mali disintegrated.

Instead of coins and gold, Ibn Battuta received three loaves of bread, a piece of beef fried in oil, and yogurt—far less generous than Mansa Musa's offerings. Ibn Battuta laughed and informed the king of the mistake. Then Mansa Sulayman provided him with a house and an allowance. When Ibn Battuta left Mali in February 1353, he received one hundred mithqals of gold.

Fractures in the ruling dynasty were becoming evident. Ibn Battuta wrote of an episode concerning Mansa Sulayman's chief wife, Qasa, the daughter of an uncle on his father's side of the family. She was considered the royal queen, a partner to the king, and her name was mentioned together with that of Sulayman's. But the king imprisoned her and replaced her with another wife, Banju, who was not a king's daughter. The people of Mali did not approve of his actions, and the chiefs spoke on Qasa's behalf. Mansa Sulayman listened to his chiefs, but he maintained that

Qasa had committed a capital crime. One of Qasa's slaves was brought forward, her hands and legs bound in chains. She was told to say what she knew. The slave said that Qasa had sent her to the king's cousin encouraging him to overthrow the king, with the support of herself and her husband's armies. Upon hearing this, the chiefs exclaimed that Qasa deserved death. Sulayman was thus just able to deter a coup.

CIVIL WAR BREAKS OUT

Mansa Sulayman reigned for twenty-four years. He and his brother, Mansa Musa, both brought the empire of Mali to its greatest points. When he died, civil war broke out between his line and that of Mansa Musa. His son Qasa succeeded him, but he died nine months later, which suggested foul play. Mansa Magha's son Mari Diata II arose victorious from the fighting and now ascended the throne.

Mari Diata II ruled for fourteen years. However, he was considered a wicked ruler and subjected his people to tortures and tyrannies. Around 1360, he presented the sultan of the Maghreb with a giraffe. The gift caused a stir because of its markings and adornments. Ibn Khaldun related a story in which he was told that Mansa Mari Diata II ruined the empire and squandered the treasury, including a prized and rare boulder of gold. Mansa Mari Diata II offered the boulder to Egyptian traders at a price so far below its value that many considered the purchase an insult. This ruler of Mali suffered from a sleeping sickness that afflicted the aristocracy. He succumbed to the disease, circa 1373 or 1374.

THE STRUGGLE FOR POWER WEAKENS THE EMPIRE

Mansa Mari Diata II's son, Musa II, succeeded him and did away with the ways of his father. Instead, he nurtured justice and consideration of his people. But an ambitious vizier usurped the power of the throne and mobilized the army. Mansa Musa II died in 1387, and his brother Magha succeeded him. He reigned for only one year and was most likely a toy for his court officers to play with. Another vizier arose to usurp the throne. He even married Mari Diata II's widow to try to make his position seem more legitimate. But his time as ruler of Mali did not last long either.

Within a span of four generations and eighty years, a direct descendant of the mighty Sundiata came to claim the throne. By then, though, Mali no longer held the authority it once had. It had lost the ability to collect revenue from the trade caravans. The empire—all that Mansa Musa and the rulers before and after him had established—had disintegrated by the mid-sixteenth century. In the early 1500s, the outermost regions of the empire had begun to assert their independence. Around the same time, the Songhays rose up and conquered much of Mali, regaining their centers at Gao and Timbuktu. They gained control of the trade routes and the gold and salt. Songhay now became the center of learning. The Songhay Empire, like the Ghana Empire and Mali Empire before it, fell apart into fractured units after Moroccan invaders crushed the Songhays in the sixteenth century.

MANSA MUSA IN MALI TODAY

Mali never again regained the glory and strength it had under Mansa Musa's rule. Yet his influence is still felt today. Modibo Keita, the first president of an independent Mali, bore the name Keita, marking him as a descendant of the Keita ruling dynasty begun by Sundiata and carried to its fullest by Mansa Musa. Another descendant is a Malian musician, Salif Keita.

DID MALIAN EXPLORERS DISCOVER AMERICA BEFORE COLUMBUS?

Some historians seem to think so. A four-teenth-century Egyptian scholar and historian described Malian explorations of the Atlantic Ocean in his book, *Roadways for Those Who Have Sight and Are Searching, in the Provinces of the Kingdoms*. There is scientific evidence that supports the possibility of contact between Africa and America. African sculptures found in the West Indies resembled those in western Africa. More artifacts were found in Brazil that seemed to have western African influences. Although the question is still debated, the planning and forethought to go into such an expedition would most likely have occurred during Mansa Musa's reign. The Mali Empire did touch on the Atlantic, and Mansa Musa's predecessor on the throne did set out on an Atlantic journey to find its end, or so Mansa Musa had said, according to al-Umari's writings. But then Mansa Musa was given to telling tall tales.

Had he lived in Mansa Musa's time, however, he would never have been allowed to be a singer or griot. According to the caste system, that role would have been far beneath him. He has developed a sound combining traditional African instruments with sounds from around the world, including jazz, pop, and even salsa. He frequently features children in his songs.

Of all the historic places in Mali today, the commercial and cultural center of Timbuktu stands out as a reminder of Mansa Musa's influence. UNESCO maintains a website to publicize the need to keep Mali's heritage safe and invites visitors to donate money to keep the mosques, including the Djinguereber Mosque and the Sankore Mosque, which are open to the public. In 1961, the year after Mali gained its independence from France, it issued two airmail stamps that paid

A descendant of Mansa Musa, musician Salif Keita combines African instruments with the music of other cultures to create a truly global sound.

homage to Mansa Musa's achievements. One stamp illustrated the Sankore Mosque.

Mansa Musa's urban traditions persevere, and Islam remains an integral part of the fabric of Mali. Through Mansa Musa, the name Mali became known far and wide. Both a strong leader to his people and an international ambassador, Mansa Musa gave Mali some of its most enduring legacies.

TIMELINE

600 CE The Ghana Empire begins to develop. The Songhays establish markets at Gao on the Niger River.

1000 The Ghana Empire reaches its peak. The Malinkes have established the state of Kangaba by this time.

1050 Barmandana, the first Muslim king of Mali, converts to Islam.

1076 Almoravid Berbers from Morocco defeat the Empire of Ghana, and the empire declines. The Almoravid force conversion to Islam.

1100 Timbuktu is established.

Early 1200s Sumanguru, king of the Sossos, rules the fragmented Empire of Ghana and attacks Kangaba but spares Sundiata Keita's life.

1230 Sundiata becomes king of Mali.

1235–55 Sundiata builds the Empire of Mali. Gold from Mali becomes the source of gold for Islamic and European currency.

1255–70 Mansa Uli, Sundiata's son, reigns. The Mali Empire expands.

1270–74 Sundiata's second son, Wati, rules.

1274–75 Sundiata's third son, Khalifa, rules.

1275–85	Abu Bakr, Sundiata's grandson through his daughter, rules.
1280	Mansa Musa is born to Faga Laye and Nana Gongo.
1285–1300	The usurper and freed slave Sakura takes control of the kingdom and rules.
1300	Sakura dies during his return from his Mecca pilgrimage.
1300–05	Mansa Uli's son Qu rules.
1305–10	Mansa Uli's son Muhammad rules.
1310–12	Abu Bakr II rules.
1307–37	Mansa Musa, the grandson of Abu Bakr, who was the brother of Sundiata, rules. The Mali Empire doubles in size and triples in trade. Islamic influence worldwide increases.
1312	Mansa Musa makes Islam the official religion of Mali.
1324	Mansa Musa begins his pilgrimage to Mecca. Mansa Musa visits Cairo and affects the world market for gold.
1325–54	North African geographer and scholar Ibn Battuta travels around the East and Africa.

1327	Mansa Musa has architect es-Saheli build mosques in the captured Songhay cities of Gao and Timbuktu.
1332	Timbuktu is raided.
1337	Mansa Musa reportedly dies.
1337–41	Mansa Musa's son, Magha, rules.
1341–60	Mansa Musa's brother, Sulayman, rules.
1375–1400	The Songhays assert independence.
1382	Mansa Musa II's death ushers in a succession crisis, leading to a weakening of the Mali Empire.
1400–80	The Empire of Mali is pressured by the Songhays and Tuaregs. The northern province breaks away. Djenné and Timbuktu assert independence. Mali's power declines further.
1471	The Portuguese arrive in western Africa.
1493–95	An ambassador of the Portuguese king visits Mansa Mamudu.
1590–1600	The Empire of Mali collapses.

Andalusia A region in southern Spain between the Mediterranean and the Atlantic Ocean that was overtaken by the Moors.

Bedouin A member of a nomadic tribe living in the Sahara.

Berber A member of a northern African tribe living in the Sahara.

dinar A unit of money used in North Africa and elsewhere.

dyeli An ancient Malian court official who also served as griot and spokesperson.

griot A person in western Africa with the responsibility to safeguard oral history through stories and poems.

hajj The pilgrimage to Mecca that a Muslim is expected to make at least once in a lifetime.

hajji An honorific title given to one who has made the pilgrimage to the Holy City of Mecca, following the fifth Pillar of Islam.

infidel A person who does not accept the Islamic faith.

Maghreb The area of northern Africa that borders the Mediterranean Sea.

Mandingo/Mandinka/Malinke Of or relating to members of the founding peoples of the Empire of Mali.

minaret A tower with a balcony that is part of a mosque. Muslims are called to prayer from the balcony.

mithqal A unit of weight for gold or a coin of gold used for gifts or payment, weighing 4.5 grams or about 1.5 tenths of an ounce.

Moor A Muslim of mixed Berber and Arab descent inhabiting northwest Africa; also a member of this group who invaded Spain in the eighth century and occupied it until 1492.

mosque A Muslim temple or place of public worship.

pagan Relating to a religion that is polytheistic or one that does not relate to teachings of the Bible.

patrilineal A line of descent through the father.

prostrate To lay oneself flat on the ground in humility.

Quran The sacred text of Islam that serves as the foundation for Islamic religion, culture, and law.

Sahel The northernmost part of the savanna that forms the transitional area between the Sahara and the wet grasslands.

savanna A long stretch of grasslands.

shahada The first of the five Pillars of Islam and the Muslim expression of faith.

sharif A descendant of the Prophet Muhammad.

Sosso A member of the group of people who conquered the Empire of Ghana and battled unsuccessfully with Sundiata Keita.

Sudan A region in Africa south of the Sahara that extends from the Atlantic Ocean to the Red Sea.

sultan A leader of an Islamic state.

Tuareg A member of the Sahara nomads.

usurp To seize power with a legal right.

vizier A high official in Muslim countries who advises the ruler and serves often as a minister of state.

The Africa Center
1280 Fifth Avenue
New York, NY 10029
(212) 444-9795
Website: https://www.theafricacenter.org
The Africa Center is a nonprofit institution that fos-
ters engagement with contemporary Africa. Its
goal is to transform understanding of the world's
oldest continent through the arts, education, and
policy research.

African Studies Association
Rutgers University—Livingston Campus
54 Joyce Kilmer Avenue
Piscataway, NJ 08854-8045
(848) 445-8173
Website: http://www.africanstudies.org
The African Studies Association is a professional
organization with nearly two thousand individual
and institutional members around the world. Its
main goal is to share information about Africa's
past and present.

Art Gallery of Ontario
317 Dundas Street West
Toronto, ON M5T 1G4

Canada
(877) 225-4246
Website: http://www.ago.net
The Art Gallery of Ontario houses one of the largest
  collections of African art in Canada. Visitors can
  also view art from other parts of the world.

Canadian Association of African Studies
Institute of African Studies
439 Paterson Hall
1125 Colonel by Drive
Carleton University
Ottawa, ON K1S 5B6
Canada
(613) 520-2600 x 2220
Website: http://caas-acea.org/caas/about-caas
The Canadian Association of African Studies is an
  organization of scholars with a mission to pro-
  mote the study of Africa in Canada and to make
  Canadians more aware of the problems and aspi-
  rations of Africans.

Metropolitan Museum of Art
1000 Fifth Avenue
New York, NY 10028
(212) 535-7710

Website: http://www.metmuseum.org

The Metropolitan Museum of Art features art and artifacts from the ancient world, including numerous artifacts from the Empire of Mali.

National Museum of African Art
950 Independence Avenue SW
Washington, DC 20013
(202) 633-1000
Website: http://africa.si.edu

The Smithsonian Institution's National Museum of African Art highlights various collections from Africa's past.

WEBSITES

Because of the changing nature of Internet links, Rosen Publishing has developed an online list of websites related to the subject of this book. This site is updated regularly. Please use this link to access this list:

http://www.rosenlinks.com/SRGT/musa

FOR FURTHER READING

Aloian, Molly. *The Sahara Desert.* New York, NY: Crabtree, 2013.

Al-Sadi, Abd, and Octave Houdas, trans. *Mansa Musa and the Mali Empire: From Tarikh al-Sudan.* Amazon Digital Services, 2015.

Chu, Daniel, and Elliott Skinner. *A Glorious Age in Africa: The Story of Three Great African Empires.* Trenton, NJ: Africa World Press, 1996.

De Villiers, Marq, and Sheila Hirtle. *Timbuktu: The Sahara's Fabled City of Gold.* New York, NY: Walker & Co., 2007.

Haywood, John. *West African Kingdoms.* Chicago, IL: Raintree, 2008.

Irwin, Florence. *The Road to Mecca.* London, England: Forgotten Books, 2015.

McKenna, Amy, ed. *The History of Western Africa.* New York, NY: Britannica Educational Publishing, 2011.

McKissack, Patricia and Fredrick McKissack. *The Royal Kingdoms of Ghana, Mali, and Songhay: Life in Medieval Africa.* New York, NY: Henry Holt, 1994.

National Geographic. *1001 Inventions and Awesome Facts from Muslim Civilization.* Washington, DC: National Geographic Kids, 2012.

Niani, D. T. *Sundiata: An Epic of Old Mali.* Harlow, England: Pearson Longman, 2006.

Nwanunobi, C. Onyeka. *Malinke*. New York, NY: Rosen, 1996.

Oliver, P. James. *Mansa Musa and the Empire of Mali*. CreateSpace Independent Publishing, 2013.

Quigley, Mary. *Ancient West African Kingdoms: Ghana, Mali, and Songhai*. Philadelphia, PA: Heinemann, 2002.

Raskin, Lawrie, and Debora Pearson. *52 Days by Camel: My Sahara Adventure*. Toronto, ON, Canada: Annick Press, 2008.

Reece, Katherine E. *West African Kingdom: Empires of Gold and Trade*. Vero Beach, FL: Rourke, 2006.

Samuels, Charlie. *Timeline of the Muslim World*. New York, NY: Gareth Stevens, 2010.

Shuter, Jane. *Ancient West African Kingdoms*. Philadelphia, PA: Heinemann, 2008.

Winters, Clyde. *African Empires in Ancient America*. Amazon Digital Services, 2013.

Wolny, Philip. *Discovering the Empire of Mali*. New York, NY: Rosen, 2014.

Zamosky, Lisa. *Mansa Musa: Leader of Mali*. Huntington Beach, CA: Teacher Created Materials, 2007.

BIBLIOGRAPHY

Abercrombie, Thomas J. "Ibn Battuta: Prince of Travelers." *National Geographic,* December 1991, pp. 2–49.

Ahmed, Nazeer. "The History of Islam: Mansa Musa." Retrieved November 30, 2015. (http://historyofislam.com/mansa-musa/).

Ajayi, J.F.A., and Michael Crowder. *History of West Africa,* Volume I. New York, NY: Columbia University Press, 1976.

Amin, Mohamed. *Journey of a Lifetime: Pilgrimage to Makkah.* Nairobi, Kenya: Camerapix Publishers International, 2000.

Appiah, Kwame Anthony, and Henry Louis Gates Jr., eds. *Africana: The Encyclopedia of the African and the African American Experience.* New York, NY: Basic Books, 1999.

Atalebe, Stephen. "Mansa Musa, the Hero." *New African,* January 2011, p. 65.

Austen, Ralph A. *Trans-Saharan Africa in World History.* New York, NY: Oxford University Press, 2010.

Bell, Nawal Morcos. "The Age of Mansa Musa of Mali: Problems in Succession and Chronology." *International Journal of African Historical Studies,* Vol. 5, No. 2, 1972, pp. 221–234.

Conrad, David C. "A Town Called Dakajalan: The Sunjata Tradition and the Question of Ancient

Mali's Capital." *Journal of African History,* Vol. 35, No. 3, 1994, pp. 355–377.

Davidson, Basil. *The African Past: Chronicles from Antiquity to Modern Times.* Boston, MA: Little Brown, 1964.

DeGraft-Johnson, J. C. *African Glory: The Story of Vanished Negro Civilizations.* London, England: Praeger, 1954.

Diop, Cheikh Anta, and Harold Salemson, trans. *Precolonial Black Africa.* Brooklyn, NY: Lawrence Hill Books, 1987.

Fage, J. D. *A History of Africa.* New York, NY: Alfred A. Knopf, 1979.

Fage, J. D. *An Introduction to the History of West Africa.* Cambridge, England: Cambridge University Press, 1962.

Goodwin, A. J. H. "The Medieval Empire of Ghana." *South African Archaeological Bulletin,* Vol. 12, No. 47, September 1957, pp. 108–112.

Hill, Margari. "The Spread of Islam in West Africa." Retrieved November 29, 2015 (http://spice.fsi .stanford.edu/docs/the_spread_of_islam_in _west_africa_containment_mixing_and _reform_from_the_eighth_to_the_twentieth _century).

Hopkins, J. F. P., trans. *Corpus of Early Arabic Sources for West African History.* Princeton, NJ: Markus Wiener Publishers, 2000.

Hunwick, John O. "The Influence of Arabic in West Africa: A Preliminary Historical Survey." *Transactions of the Historical Society of Ghana* Vol. 7, 1964, pp. 24–41.

Lomeie, Roman. *Muslim Societies in Africa: A Historical Anthropology.* Bloomington, IN: Indiana University Press, 2013.

Stearns, Peter N. *The Encyclopedia of World History.* Boston, MA, and New York, NY: Houghton Mifflin, 2001.

Van Sertima, Ivan. *They Came Before Columbus: The African Presence in Ancient America.* New York, NY: Random House, 2003.

INDEX

ABOUT THE AUTHOR

Barbara Krasner teaches creative writing and children's literature at a local university in New Jersey. She is the author of more than fifteen books for young readers. Her interest in ancient history dates back to the fourth grade.

PHOTO CREDITS

Cover (portrait – detail from decorated map), pp. 82-83 Abraham Cresques/ Getty Images; cover (map) Heritage Images/Hulton Archive/Getty Images; pp. 5, 21 Private Collection / © Look and Learn/Bridgeman Images; pp. 10-11 Pictures from History/Bridgeman Images; pp. 12, 33, 61, 86-87 Werner Forman/Universal Images Group/Getty Images; p. 18 SSPL/Getty Images; p. 23 Francois Xavier Marit/AFP/Getty Images; p. 27 James L. Stanfield/National Geographic Image Collection/Getty Images; p. 34 Xavier Rossi/Gamma-Rapho/Getty Images; p. 39 Print Collector/Hulton Archive/Getty Images; pp. 40-41 Florilegius/SSPL/Getty Images; p. 45 Giuglio Gil/hemis.fr/Getty Images; pp. 48-49 Alinari Archives/Getty Images; p. 51 Gary Yeowell/Photolibrary/ Getty Images; pp. 54-55 Issam Madkouk/arabianEye/Getty Images; p. 59 © Christine Osborne Pictures/Alamy Stock Photo; p. 63 Sean Caffrey/Lonely Planet Images/Getty Images; p. 66 Ariadne Van Zandbergen/Lonely Planet Images/Getty Images; p. 69 Amar Grover/AWL Images/Getty Images; p. 73 Photo12/Universal Images Group/Getty Images; pp. 76-77 © akg-images/ The Image Works, Inc.; p. 80 Culture Club/Hulton Archive/Getty Images; pp. 92-93 Simon Maina/AFP/Getty Images

Designer: Michael Moy; Editor: Shalini Saxena; Photo Researcher: Bruce Donnola